Clicker Training the Law of Attraction

or

How to treat the Universe like a Dog

by Anna G. Shiney

AdlA

Clicker training the law of attraction or
How to treat the universe like a dog
by Anna G. Shiney

AdlA Papageienhilfe gGmbH
Neckarstrasse 23
D-65795 Hattersheim
Germany
+49-6145-548-285
+49-6145-548-286 (fax)
www.annashiney.com

To report errors, please send a note to info@annashiney.com

ISBN-13: 978-3-939770-27-5

Layout: Anna G. Shiney
Front cover: Annie Anderson, www.asamediagroup.com
Back cover: Annie Anderson / Anna G. Shiney
Clipart: www.karenswhimsy.com, www.webweaver.nu

Table of Content

1. Preamble

The law of attraction promises to turn your life into a magical fulfillment of your wildest dreams. If you could only do it. In spite of abundant literature, CDs and DVDs on the subject, the reality for many of us is that our manifestation results leave a lot to be desired. And so it was for me.

A big part of the problem was that the materials I reviewed were vague in their instructions or terribly complicated or both. They told me „what“ I needed to do, but failed to enlighten me on the „how“. In addition, the „what“ seemed rather impossible to me, as well. According to the materials, manifestation required the total control of my mind: control of what

I was thinking and feeling - and even what my subconscious was thinking and feeling. My reality, however, was that most of the time I didn't even know what I was thinking or feeling, let alone being able to control it. While these instructions seemed to work for those people who were selling the programs, as evidenced by photos of them in front of big houses, big cars or aboard yachts, this certainly did not work for me. It just made me feel frustrated, incapable and inadequate. Consequently, my manifestation results were awful. My desires, however, remained big. My life was a mess. Everything that could go wrong did go wrong. I was non-stop busy, overwhelmed and exhausted trying to beat out the latest fire, reacting, as one problem after another slugged me. Every time I thought, „it can't get worse than this", it did. I was despairing.

But then my personal breakthrough came: I was driving home from grocery shopping listening to an audio book on manifesting, when it suddenly occurred to me that the message I heard over and over in all those programs reminded me strongly of clicker training, an animal training method I was well familiar with from practicing and teaching it for many years. All of a sudden, what I had to do became completely clear to me. The universe wanted - no needed - to be treated like a dog. To train it, I only needed to lavish attention on what I wanted and ignore the unwanted. Could it really be this easy? I started to pay attention to the many good things the universe was giving me every day and reinforced this by thanking and loving the universe for them. At the same time, I completely ignored the monkey wrenches in my life. After a while this became second nature to me. It certainly made me feel much happier. But, even better, it worked! It really, really worked! At last, I was manifesting successfully. Step by step I clicker trained the universe out of the mess my life was and transformed it to consist increasingly of beautiful circumstances in which I felt peaceful, happy and in control.

Clicker training the universe was my personal breakthrough to implementing the law of attraction in my life and become a successful manifester. Maybe, hopefully, it will be yours, too. Clicker training the universe is as easy as clicker training any animal. If you have ever trained an animal, this will be easy for you. But even if you have not, don‘t despair. Clicker training is so easy to learn. In this book I will show you exactly what to do and how to do it.

Enjoy and have fun training,

Anna Shiney.

2. Behavior, training and the law of attraction

Before we can begin with training, you need to have a basic understanding about how behavior is formed. With this knowledge, the principles and applications of clicker training may be more easily grasped and applied.

Behavior and how it is formed

Every living being, regardless of whether it is wild or tame, human, animal or even the universe, will over time exhibit only behaviors that are in one way or another rewarding to it. For example, you keep going to work only if you get paid with money or some other reward, like appreciation. If your employer fails to pay you month after month, you will eventually stop working for him. Your behavior - going to work - was not being reinforced, so after a while you stopped showing it. If, on the other hand, your employer was rewarding you for sitting at your desk, but did not reward you for time spent visiting customers, you would spend a lot more time sitting at your desk and minimize customer visits. Thus, behavior is formed by the way rewards are given.

Your dog behaves the same way. She will retrieve objects, for example, for treats or praise and will stop retrieving if your reactions are not worthwhile to her. If you want her to retrieve only a particular item, it gets even more tricky. Say you want her to bring you a yellow ball. She runs off and brings you a green ball. You do not reward her for this - after all you wanted a yellow ball. Maybe, you will even scold her. Confused, your dog runs off and brings you a blue ball. Again - no reward. After all, you wanted her to bring you the yellow ball.

She then runs and gets you the red ball. Again, you ignore her. It is the yellow ball, you want. Confused and frustrated your dog gives up and goes for a nap. Now it is your turn to be really frustrated. Stupid,

stupid dog. She is so stubborn, never listens, never brings you what you want. You'll just stop asking her to do anything for you at all. Maybe you should just give her away. No one can live with a dog that does not listen. A few weeks later you bump into your former dog and her new owner in the park. You cannot believe your eyes. She retrieves upon command not only the yellow ball, but also the blue ball and the red ball. This is so unfair! After all, you tried so hard to train her. And her new owner, seemingly without effort, can make her do anything he wants.

Oh no, this probably means that you are a bad person and just don't deserve to have an obedient dog. Or you are just too stupid to train a dumb dog.

You are laughing? Yet, this is - unfortunately - exactly the way many of us are dealing with the universe. Should it be surprising then that we don't manifest?

Had you been an experienced trainer, the story between you and your dog would have unfolded completely different and more joyful for both of you. A good trainer sets his pupil up for success. A good trainer will catch his dog whenever she does anything right and rewards that. Over time, the animal does more and more things right and becomes a sheer joy to live with. It is then fairly easy to shape her towards specific goals. Had you rewarded your dog for bringing you any of the balls, she would have learned to happily retrieve for you anytime you asked. Once she had learned this, you would acknowledge your dog bringing any ball. But, if she retrieved the yellow ball for you, she'd be celebrated like a star and been given a jackpot of treats. Now, how long do you think it would have taken for her to learn to bring you the yellow ball more often? Like a dog, the universe will joyfully retrieve for you whatever you want, whenever you want, if you treat it like a good trainer should.

What is clicker training?

Training is most successful when you are able to reinforce exactly the behavior that you want your dog to show more often. The more precise the timing of your rewards is, the faster the animal will learn the wanted behavior. In real life, however, it is often impossible to give a reward at exactly the same time that a behavior is shown. This impedes learning, as the animal does not know what he is being rewarded for when the treat does not coincide with the desired behavior. Here is where the clicker comes to the rescue.

The clicker is a little tool that makes a click sound when activated. In a process, called conditioning, the clicker is linked to a reward. The animal learns that upon the sound of the click it will receive a treat.

Once the clicker has been thus conditioned, the trainer can use it to mark the wanted behavior precisely when it happens while having a few seconds time afterward to actually deliver the reward. Due to this precision, the trainer can clearly communicate to the animal which one of its behaviors garnered the reward. Thus, training results are achieved more quickly and easily with clicker training than with any other training method.

Why no punishment?

In clicker training we focus on positive reinforcement of desired behavior. Unwanted behavior is ignored instead of punished. Punishment is avoided, as it may inadvertently act as a reinforcer of unwanted behaviors (apart from the ethical implications, of course). For example, imagine a dog sitting outside the door. When it scratches and whines, you yell: „No! Shut up“. Will this stop the dog from scratching the door and whining? Not at all. The reality is that to the dog even negative attention is better than being ignored. It just learned, „I only need to scratch and whine, to get some attention!“

The universe behaves the same way. You can often see this when people are worried about a situation. They go „no, no, no, I don‘t want this“ in their minds. Usually, this „no“ is attached to strong emotions, such as fear. And guess what happens? Yep, the universe delivers the unwanted situation right to their doorstep, without fail, each time. So, don‘t do it. Don‘t pay any attention to unwanted situations or outcomes. Don‘t even think about them. It will just make it worse and manifest for you exactly what you do not want.

Substitution

„Don‘t do this!“, „Don‘t do that!“ I know! Not doing or not thinking about something is the hardest thing to do. Thus, we use a little trick. Instead of not thinking about an unwanted issue or outcome, we think of an outcome that we do want and that makes us feel good. Ideally, this would be an outcome that makes the undesired outcome impossible to happen. This is called substitution and is frequently used in animal training to alleviate behavior issues.

One example would be a dog barking like crazy whenever someone comes to your door. This is, of course, awfully annoying, not only to you, but also to your neighbors. If you are really unlucky, it could also get you evicted from your home. Thus, most dog owners try to shush their dogs. The dog receives a lot of attention for going ballistic when someone comes to your door. This reinforces the unwanted behavior.

A much better approach would be, for example, to teach your dog to retrieve a toy for you whenever the front door bell rings. It is impossible for him to bark at the same time, as he is carrying a toy in his snout. Problem solved.

With the universe we do the same thing. Imagine you have a rather decrepit car, but desperately need to arrive at an important appointment on time. Normally, you would worry incessantly about being late, what excuses you would make, etc. etc. What you should do instead is to imagine that you arrive fifteen minutes early in a happy and totally relaxed state of mind. Make it vivid. In your mind you could tell the receptionist, while you are waiting for your appointment to begin, about the traffic being really smooth. Talk to her about how much you love your little old beat-up car that has served you so reliable over so many years.

This is, of course, a substitution to the outcome of your car breaking down which makes that happening simply impossible. At the same time, you are also sending loads of happy energy about your car and your trip to the universe. No energy is being sent to the unwanted outcome, anymore. It really is that easy.

3. Before we begin

In order to achieve the best success in manifesting, there are several important issues we need to address before we - finally - begin with the actual clicker training of the universe.

Practice makes perfect

Manifesting is not magic. It is not reserved for some gurus. It is just another skill to learn. Like all skills, learning will be a little easier for some of you and a little harder for others. But it can be learned by all of you. Manifesting will not come to you magically just by reading a book. Like all skills, it will have to be learned by practicing. You just have to stick with this method and practice it, until it has been mastered by you.

Fear of failure

The worst thing you can do while learning to manifest, is not to do anything at all. Yet, a lot of beginners make this mistake. They want to be perfect before they even begin. Sadly, too often this means that they never begin. Another variation of this theme is beginners who start to manifest and give up when it is not working perfectly right the first time.

This is wrong! Like any skill you have to practice to learn it. You have to fall off the bicycle many times before you can ride it without training wheels. It will then take even more practice and falls before you can freestyle it. So do not give up! If your manifestations don‘t work at first or work differently from what you had expected, keep on trying. Clicker training the universe is an incredibly forgiving method and very effective once it has been learned. But you have to stick with it.

How to use this book

When you work with this book, please go through the chapters and exercises in the order given. The exercises build on one another. You need to practice each exercise thoroughly, before you move on to the next. If you rush through the basic exercises, you will have problems with the more advanced ones, later on, because you are lacking the solid manifestation foundation that would have been built by thoroughly practicing the preceding exercises.

Whenever you move to a new exercise and find it is not working for you, there is a good chance that you moved forward too quickly. In that case, go back one step in your training and practice the previously achieved level more intensively, until you have become fully proficient at it. Only then should you attempt to move on to the next exercise level.

Trainer's mood

In animal training it is a well known phenomenon that animals mirror our emotions. If you are in a bad mood and try to train animals, at best it won't work. At worst you'll get bitten. The universe is the same way. If you are upset, nothing will go right. We all know about days that start out wrong and proceed to get worse during their course. Thus, if you want to train the universe, you better get yourself centered and feeling good first. Else, you might as well not bother for all the good it is going to do. To this purpose, I recommend that you do some warm-up exercises before training, just like any athlete would. Great warm-up exercises are the love and gratitude exercises outlined in the next chapter.

Fun & playfulness

In manifesting you will receive the best results - or even any results at all - when you approach the exercises with happiness in your heart. Every exercise session should, therefore, be approached with an attitude of fun and playfulness.

Putting your nose to the grindstone and pushing on, even though you don‘t feel like it, are tired or frustrated, may be a great strategem to study for exams. It definitely does not work in training the universe. The whole book and its exercises are meant to be fun for you. They have to be fun for them to work! Any discomfort, tiredness, frustration or any other negative feelings that may crop up during training are indicators that you should take a break. Go for a walk, watch a funny movie, bake some bread, meditate. Do whatever is needed to get you into a light and positive state of mind. Only then should you continue training.

Resistance

Often when we start working with the law of attraction, we have inner resistance that sabotages our attempts at manifesting. This resistance might present itself to you as a nagging voice telling you that manifesting will not work. It might show up as a distraction every time you want to sit down to practice manifesting. Or it may lead you to forget to do your manifesting exercises, altogether. Regardless of the form in which resistance presents itself, its goal is to protect us by stopping us from even attempting to manifest. I call that resistance my inner police officer, because he wants me to stick to all the rules accumulated over time, regardless of whether they make sense or not in my present life.

Our inner police officer is not a mean guy. He is trying to protect us. Unfortunately, though, he perceives all change as being dangerous. After all, if we become rich and happy we may lose our friends, be kidnapped, become victims to fraudsters, turn into horrible persons or whatever other horror scenario our inner police officer can imagine. He is also trying to save us from disappointment should we not succeed. To him our happy self that wants to manifest is deluded, losing grip on reality and altogether too much like a hippie that will start doing drugs, join a sect or end up in prison.

Regardless of whether our inner police officer is mean or not, though, he is definitely in the way of our manifesting efforts.

Very often, he is successful, too. Beginner manifestors may easily succumb to his interferences and their manifesting efforts are failures. From this they conclude that manifesting does not work and stop. Mission accomplished for the inner police officer. If we don‘t want to fall into the same trap, we need to make manifesting non-threatening for our inner police officer.

Thus, we will start with tiny steps and easy topics which are non-threatening to even the most diligent inner police officer. That way we can slip right under his watchful eye. We will start out learning to get more of the good things we already have.

This is familiar territory for our inner police officers, known to be safe and not scary at all. Next, we will manifest little, unimportant things, such as a five dollar bill or a good parking spot. This too serves to relax our inner police officer. After that, we will gradually inch up to increasingly dramatic changes in our lifes. Hold on tight and enjoy the ride!

You are worth it!

Please! Do not feel guilty about manifesting too much or asking for too much. First of all, you, just like any other living being, are worth it. Second of all, you are manifesting every second of your life, anyway. The only difference is that you are now doing it consciously. You are finally putting some thought into your manifestations.

Instead of allowing your thoughts and feelings to flit all over the place like a loose cannon, never knowing where the next impact may end up, you are giving them direction. I believe it is vastly preferable to utilize your manifesting potential, rather than to squander it senselessly, like most of us are still doing.

4. Training treats for the universe

Appropriate training rewards are important to achieve desired behaviors. When training animals, the trainer usually performs a treat test to identify what the pupil's favorite treat is. This favorite treat is subsequently only given during training which makes the animal very keen on it. Thus, the animal is highly motivated during training, because it wants to get some of its favorite treats.

The universe's favorite treats

With the universe we don't need to do any treat testing at all. The „animal" is the same for all of us and its favorite treats are well known. The universe's favorite treats are strong feelings, regardless of whether they are positive or negative. However, as we are trying to manifest positive outcomes, we should use only positive feelings.

If we were to use negative feelings, it would be pretty hard for us to focus on positive outcomes at the same time. Instead, there would be a strong likelihood that we would focus on and manifest negative outcomes. Why would we want to risk that? Of all the positive feelings, love and gratitude are the strongest and most positive ones. Therefore, we will use these two feelings as treats when we are clicker training the universe.

Delivering the universe's favorite treat

Now that we know what our training treats are, how will we deliver them to the universe? Whenever the universe presents to us anything that we like, we need to be able to reinforce this immediately with strong feelings of love and gratitude. Thus, we need to be able to quickly and effortlessly draw on these emotions whenever and wherever we need them. This can be difficult at the best of times and seemingly impossible when we are having a miserable day. The solution to this problem is to practice conjuring up high intensity feelings of love and gratitude at will. We then attach these to a trigger word. Subsequently, the trigger word will recall the strong positive feelings of love and gratitude. Thus, we will be able to flood ourselves with these emotions just by saying or thinking the trigger word. The following exercise teaches you exactly how to do that.

Exercise 4.1: Gratitude

The gratitude exercise teaches you to generate strong feelings of gratitude when a trigger word is said or thought. It is also an excellent warm-up exercise before your manifestation training sessions.

Step 1: Generate gratitude feelings

Take a couple of deep breaths to relax. Next, recall a situation when something went surprisingly and overwhelmingly well for you. Relive that situation in your mind: Go through each aspect and review the details, until you can feel the gratitude you were feeling at that time.

Breathe deep and focus on that gratitude. Involve yourself deeply in that moment and in that feeling, until you feel you could burst with gratitude. Feel gratitude pulse and flow through your heart and your entire body.

Step 2: Attach the gratitude feelings to the trigger word

Once you are filled from head to toe with strong gratitude feelings, say „Thank you!“. Wallow in all that gratitude feeling and say „Thank you!“, again. The purpose of this is to link the gratitude feelings to the trigger phrase „Thank you!“. After some practice, just saying or thinking the trigger will automatically generate those strong gratitude feelings you have been practicing.

Now take a little pause. Take a couple of deep breaths, drink some water. Ready for the next round?

Step 3: Practice

Go back in your mind to that feeling of overwhelming gratitude, again. You will likely find it easier this time to generate that feeling. Let the gratitude build. Make the feeling stronger and bigger. And then say „Thank you“ again, while holding that feeling. Repeat this lesson three more times or so. Stop this exercise while you are feeling great. Do not make the mistake of going on and on, until you get tired. Your mind, heart and soul need to remember the great feeling, not the tired, frustrated one that you get when practicing too long.

Step 4: Practice, practice, practice

As many times, as possible during the day, conjure up that situation and those gratitude feelings. Build the vibration of that gratitude up and up, before saying „Thank you!“. You will likely find that it becomes increasingly easier for you to generate that feeling. Always remember to stop this exercise while you are feeling at the peak of your positive gratitude vibration.

Exercise 4.2: Love

Love is the other top positive emotion for training the universe. It shows the universe your full appreciation for what you have received. Therefore, you should also practice generating strong love vibrations, whenever and wherever required, regardless of distractions. Use the same method for this as you have used to practice the grateful vibration, above. Use „I love this!“ as your trigger phrase, instead of „Thank you!“.

5. *First steps: More of what we have*

We will begin our clicker training the universe by learning how to get more of the good things we already have. Like in the example of the ball retrieving dog, we will start off by rewarding the universe for all the things it is already bringing to us. This reinforces the universe for its positive actions and prompts it to give us more. At the same time, it is excellent practice for us to use our clicker and rewards correctly.

The clicker word

In training the universe, we need to tell it exactly what it is that we like. If we were training a dog, we would be using a clicker for this. With the universe, we will simply use a word instead of a clicker. This has the advantage that we always have it with us and we can also use it silently by thinking rather than saying it. I prefer being discrete about my clicker-training-the-universe activities. I mean, do you really want to explain what you are doing to your boss, colleagues or neighbors?

My preferred clicker word is „Yes!“. Like a click, it is short and precise. It also conveys the right meaning to me. If another word works better for you, such as „mine“ or „want“ or „apple“, you can feel perfectly free to use that, as well. As long as the word is short and can be applied with ease and meaning to anything or any situation that you like.

When you are training animals, the click is followed by the reward. In the case of training the universe this would be you clicking by emphatically saying „Yes!“. You would reward the universe by emphatically saying „I love it!“ and „Thank you!“ while feeling the strong positive emotions of gratitude and love associated with the reward words. The combination of clicking and rewarding is referred to as click and treat. In writing, trainers often abbreviate this as click & treat or c/t.

Exercise 5.1 Click & treat

We are now ready to start with our first clicker training exercise. Find yourself a comfortable place to sit where you won't be disturbed. Before you begin this or any other exercise, you should warm-up to raise your emotions to a positive and supportive level. The easiest way to do this is to run through exercises 4.1 and 4.2 of the previous chapter. But you can use any other method, too, as long as it makes you feel really good and positive.

All set? Great. Let's begin with the actual exercise: Look around you. Do you see anything you like? Do you feel anything that you like? Perhaps you can see your children in the yard playing peacefully, or you like the way one of your kitchen counters is completely clutter free. Maybe you are glad that your head is pain free or you are looking at a book you enjoyed reading. Just pick one item that you appreciate. It doesn't matter what it is, as long as it is something you like. As an example, I am looking at a tea light in a pink mosaic glass holder, right now. Its flame is flickering gently. It looks so nice and it makes me feel all cozy and peaceful. It is definitely something I appreciate.

Now emphatically say „Yes!“ or whichever clicker word you use. Then give the universe its rewards by saying with feeling „I love it!“ and „Thank you!“. Feel the reward emotions strongly while looking at the item you chose a little longer, enjoying it. That is all. Really easy - wouldn‘t you agree? By the way, it does not matter whether you say the words out loud or think them. The emotions are what matters. So when you think or say „Yes!“ you must mean it with all your heart. And the rewards must, as we had previously practiced, carry with them strong positive emotions.

Now look around the room again. Do you see anything else that you like? Focus on it, say „Yes!“, or whatever clicker word you are using. Reward the universe with „I love it!“ and „Thank you!“. Feel the reward emotions strongly. Enjoy looking at the item and feeling the positive energy for a little longer. Continue like this around the room. Please remember to stop before you get tired or bored. Manifesting is all about feeling good and having fun.

You may practice this exercise - or variations of it - daily, to show the universe that you do appreciate all that it does for you.

Exercise 5.2: Daily gratitude list

Many people who manifest make a daily list of things that they are grateful for. I strongly recommend that you also get into this habit. It does not have to be a long list: Three to five items are fully sufficient. Here is how to do it:

- Do your warm up exercises
- Think of five things you are grateful for in your life
- Write them down
- View the first item on the list and click & treat it with all the positive emotions you can muster
- Enjoy the item and the feeling associated with it for a little while
- Then move to the next item on your list. Click & treat, as before
- Continue, one by one with each item on your list, until each has been click & treated

Try to put different items on your list every day. You will come to see just how much the universe has already brought into your life that you can be really grateful for. If you perform this ritual at night, just before you go to sleep, all these positive feelings will be carried into the sleep state with you and can continue to work all night for you. If you do this in the morning, the positive feelings will help you get a good start into the day.

Exercise 5.3: Grazing

Grazing refers to the feeding behavior of some animals. They go along their way and nibble here and there a little bit rather than having one big meal. Clicker training the universe really lends itself to grazing. Rather than having only formal training sessions, you can graze all day at the myriad of wonderful things the universe presents to you by actively noticing and click & treating them. This will help you manifest much easier, as you will be in a positive state of mind for a large part of the day and not only during training sessions. Those positive feelings you carry with you all day will pull in more and more positive experiences for you, as you go along.

Great opportunities for grazing present themselves many times during the day. You could use commuting time when you are driving to work, going to school, grocery shopping or on your way to visiting a client. For example, when you are on your way to work you can click & treat traffic lights changing in time for you, beautiful foliage on trees, the first flowers of spring, a stranger smiling at you. Opportunities abound. And it is such an excellent way to start the day. All those positive feelings you have been generating while going to work or school will massively help you towards having a great day.

Other opportunities for grazing are during office breaks, in boring meetings, while waiting in line at the grocery store and of course when commuting back home. You‘d be surprised how pleasantly you can while away time whilst grazing the universe‘s daily gifts to you. Soon you will notice the universe delivering more and more presents to you.

Exercise 5.4: Reminders

One variation of grazing is to use reminders for items you wish to manifest more of. In this you behave like an animal that grazes, but will only eat a certain type of berry. Thus, whenever it sees one of those berries, it will eat it and ignore all the berries it does not want. As an example, let‘s use money. Couldn‘t we all use a little more of that? In this exercise you will start to pay attention to all the times during the day that you handle money in any way shape or form and click & treat that. Integrating the money reminder exercise into your daily routine, your day could unfold as follows:

Before you leave the house in the morning, you quickly check your wallet to see how much is in there. Only ten dollars left, you make a mental note to go to the cash machine. Before you put your wallet away, you look at the ten dollars, affirm them with an emphatic „Yes!“, before rewarding the universe with emotionally charged „I love it!“ and „Thank you!“. As you leave your home you still feel happy about your ten dollars.

Next you stop by a coffee shop to pick-up a coffee and a muffin. You give the cashier your ten dollar bill, after click & treating it in the wink of a second that it took to pull it out of the wallet and hand it over. As the cashier gives you the change you look at it, as if to check it, but instead you click & treat the coins you are holding in your hand before putting them in your pocket.

As you are rushing down the street, you see a penny glinting in the sunlight. Of course you pick it up, delighted, that the universe is already reacting to your affirmations and giving you a little money present. Buoyed by this sign that the universe is listening, you click & treat the penny with supercharged positive energy.

You stop by the instant teller and withdraw some money. As the machine delivers you accept the crisp new bank notes into your hand pleased about the way they look, feel and smell. Of course you take a moment to click & treat the universe for that. You continue on your way and pass a beggar sitting in the street with a change cup. You stop to give him some of your change and, smiling, you include your lucky penny, sending him some of your luck and happiness with it. As you drop the coins into his paper cup you quickly click & treat them, still smiling about the happiness it brings you to share your abundance with another soul. He gave you the chance to feel affluent, caring, happy about the money you have, kind and all kinds of other positive feelings. With a big smile on your face you continue on your way.

As you enter your office building you notice an advertisement for the lottery depicting huge amounts of money. Smilingly you click & treat that as well. As you sit down at your desk you notice some loose change that has been lying there for ages. Of course, you click & treat it. Frequently during the day your eyes will roam to those coins and you will start to smile to yourself as you click & treat those coins again and again. You are meeting a friend for lunch. At the restaurant you pay with your credit card. You click & treat having that credit card and also the bill. You love and are grateful that you are able to go out for lunch and pay that bill.

After lunch you go online to buy a birthday present for a friend. You decidc to pay with Paypal. Is that money, you ask yourself? It surely is. Thus you click & treat the amount shown, before you hit the confirmation button. While you are still on the internet, you log into your online bank account and check the balance which you also click & treat.

In the evening you take care of some personal finances, paying some bills. Each check you write you click & treat, feeling grateful that you have the money to pay your bills. If you are only making minimum payments that is fine, too. Be happy and grateful that you have the money to pay those.

Sounds exhausting? Initially it can be a bit of a challenge for some of you to remember to click & treat all forms of money you come into contact with. It can also be a challenge to remain positive, rather than complaining about how expensive „everything" has become. But, if you stick with it, practice being affirmative and positive, click & treating the universe whenever you come into contact with money, then soon it will become second nature. And you will be happy about money a lot. Just seeing it will make you smile, because you so frequently connect strong positive emotions with it. The results of click & treating money frequently and feeling so good about it will be reflected in your personal finances.

6. Improving

In the previous chapter we focused on getting more of something the universe is already delivering to us. One variation of this is to improve those things the universe has provided us with. We do this by focussing on the good and ignoring the bad traits of just about anything.

One great area for this is relationships. The term relationship is loosely defined here. Apart from significant others, family members, friends, acquaintances, bosses, colleagues, pets and so on, we also have relationships with our cars, computers, homes, our own bodies and so forth. The quality of these relationships may range from nearly perfect to disastrous. It does not have to be like that, though. Any relationship, no matter how bad, can be improved with a little bit of clicker training.

Exercise 6.1: Improving relationships

You can do this exercise on any person you chose. As an example, I will be showing you how to use this exercise on a difficult boss. Feel free, though, to use it on any other person in your life that you are having problems with.

I find it hard to beat a difficult boss on the list of things that can truly make your life miserable. You cannot escape him, cannot quit, because you need the money and he has the power. Or does he? Following the law of attraction, my answer would be „no“. You have the power to manifest the transformation of this relationship in a way that makes it pleasant for you or that removes your boss from your surroundings.

I am sure, you are well aware of those aspects of your boss that you don‘t like, such as his harsh manners, perpetual bad mood, claiming your accomplishments as his, to just name a few. But have you ever considered what may be good about him? That is exactly what I would like you to do right now. Let‘s start by doing the warm up exercises so you are in a positive mind set. Grab some paper and a pen and get comfortable. Now start making a list of you boss' positive aspects. This may seem awfully hard at first. Make it easy on yourself by starting with really simple things, such as: He showers, before he comes to work. See I have you laughing already. That is the idea! Keep it light and fluffy at first. You can always dig deeper later on, after you have softened up a bit towards him. Other examples might be:

- He wears nice shoes, a nice shirt, clean socks
- He wears awful cloths, making you feel well dressed
- He keeps his desk tidy
- He keeps his desk messy, allowing you to be less than perfect, as well
- He goes for long lunches, so you have time away from him each day
- He has a photo of his family on his desk
- He has no photo of his family on his desk

Once you have written down your list of positive aspects, go through the list one-by-one, getting in touch with your happiness about each point and click & treating it.

After you have gone through the list in this way, you should be feeling a bit more charitable about your boss. Now think of him again and consider, if you can find anything else that is positive about him. Things that come up now may be a bit more personal than before. This happens, because you have to some degree opened up to him emotionally through the first round of this exercise. Positive aspects that you may notice now could include:

- He loves his kid
- He loves his dog
- He is understanding when your kid is ill
- He gets enthusiastic about playoff results
- He handles difficult clients well

Once you have written down every additional positive aspect that comes to mind, run through click & treating each new item on the list, just like we did in the first round. I would suggest you do this briefly twice a day. Once on your way home to bring into focus anything good you experienced with your boss that day. This will make it easier for you to have a nice and relaxed evening. Doing this exercise is vastly preferable to spending your precious private time going through all kinds of grievances in your mind which will only pull you down.

The second time you do the exercise should be in the morning. This will set-off your day and your interactions with your boss to a good start. Remember to add the positive aspects from the day before to your master list. If you stick with it, you will find that your boss becomes better and better and much easier to deal with.

Quite often though, this exercise will lead to your boss simply disappearing from your life. It seems, some people thrive on negative energy. As you remember, to focus on the positive, you will be less upset by him and no longer feeding him negative energy. In order to obtain the negative energy he craves, the difficult boss has to move on. This can be a very nice side effect of the improving exercise and it seems to happen fairly frequently.

Exercise 6.2: Improving health

Manifesting may also be used on health issues. There are basically two methods you can use for this. Visualizing being healthy and focusing on those parts of you that are healthy. In this exercise, we will do the latter.

As an example, assume that you have a piercing headache on the left hand side of your head, but the right hand side of your head is fine and pain free. What you do is to focus your attention on the pain free side of your head. As in the previous exercises, you click it by emphatically saying „Yes!“, followed by „I love it!" and „Thank you!" coupled with their strong positive emotions. Keep focussing on the well side of your head while holding the positive feelings.

Another example is the treatment of little injuries, such as a stubbed toe. But you may also use this exercise for more severe conditions. For these, I would recommend that you work with lists, again. Enumerate all parts of your body that are healthy and pain free. Write them down. Then go through the list item by item, affirming each and click & treating it. Remember to keep your focus on each items while feeling the strong positive emotions associated with the reward phrases. Keep going, until your toe feels better.

Manifesting can also be used for more significant illnesses than a stubbed toe. But please, use your common sense and see a physician first. These exercises are not meant to replace proper medical care. Rather view them as augmentation of and support during treatment.

7. Something new

So far you have practiced catching the universe doing something right, by click & treating that. You have learned to generate strong feelings of love and gratitude at will. And you should be well on the way to incorporating love and gratitude into your day, as it unfolds - every day. This means you are ready. Ready to start manifesting something new. Let‘s start with something small, so we won‘t startle your inner police officer into action. How about a five dollar bill? That‘s not threatening.

Starting manifesting with something „small“, such as a five dollar bill has other advantages, as well.

Many of us perceive it to be easier to manifest something „small" than something „big". Thus, starting with something „small" reduces the danger of you getting into your own way with negative thoughts, such as „It will never work", „What are you dreaming of", and the like. It is easy for you to believe that you will indeed hold a five dollar bill in your hands. Since five dollars is not exactly a huge amount of money, it makes is easier for you to detach yourself from the outcome of the manifestation. If it doesn't work - so what. You will simply try again. Right here, with our little five dollar bill, we have learned several secrets to successful manifesting:

- Get the inner police officer out of the way
- Prevent negative thoughts from interfering
- Detach yourself from the outcome
- Believe that your manifestation is possible.

Exercise 7.1: Simple objects - Manifesting a five dollar bill

Have you found a comfortable seat where you will not be disturbed? Have you done your warm-up exercises? Great. Let's begin. Close your eyes and imagine holding a five dollar bill in your hands. Look at it closely in your mind. Turn it over and look at its back. Rub it between your fingers. Feel the texture. The crinkliness of the paper. Get your senses involved. Smell the mustiness of a used bill. Or is it a new one smelling of ink? Can you hear the sound of it being rubbed between your fingers? Is it as real to you, as it would be, if you held a real five dollar bill in your hands? When you have achieved that point, I want you feel really pleased about holding the five dollar bill in your hands. Smile and be happy about having that five dollar bill. Then click & treat it: „Yes!“, „I love it!“ and „Thank you!“.

Open your eyes and forget about it. Go and do something else. This is called „letting go“. It is an important part of successful manifesting to let go of the outcome. If you keep thinking about the outcome, you are prone to send energy to negative thoughts such as „I wonder if I can do this.“ „Oh, I think this is not going to happen.“ etc. Thus, it is best to simply forget about it and get on with your daily life.

Building your manifesting muscle

Successful manifesting has a lot to do with believing. You need to believe that it is possible, before anything - no matter how „big“ or „small“ - can be manifested by you. Although it is not correct, many of us believe, that it is easier to manifest a five dollar bill than a cheque over $1,000,000. To the universe it is the same - it is energy. But you have to believe that you can manifest it, before you can create any amount of money in your reality. Since I want to make manifesting really easy for you, we will train within the context of this believe system, until you have outgrown it. This is one of the reasons why we start our manifesting exercise with a five dollar bill.

Once you have manifested your five dollar bill from the previous exercise, do it again. And once you have done so, manifest yet another five dollar bill. Do you have any idea, how often you have to train an exercise with your dog, before he is one hundred percent firm on it? Training the universe is no different. Repetition makes the master.

Continue manifesting five dollar bills, until it becomes as easy to you as buying a loaf of bread at the bakery. When you buy bread, you ask the baker for it with no doubt in your mind that he will give you the loaf of bread. And of course, without fail, he gives you the bread you asked for. Similarly, you ask the universe for a five dollar bill and it is given to you.

Once manifesting a five dollar bill is as easy for you as asking for that loaf of bread, you are ready to move one step up. Manifest a ten dollar bill. Practice that, until it becomes second nature to you, too. Then move up to twenty dollars, then fifty dollars, then one hundred dollars. If you would like to and if it makes manifesting easier for you, you may, of course, also imagine a cheque. Do whatever makes manifesting easy for you. Each successful manifestation is like money in your training account. The more of this success currency you have in your bank, the easier manifesting will become for you. Your ability to believe is supported by all your previous success stories. So keep collecting them.

Of course, manifesting is not only good for obtaining money. Other easy exercises for you to practice are perfect parking spots, catching a train you are late for, getting a seat for a show that is booked out, etc. Play with it. Have fun with it. You will see, the more you use it, the better you get at manifesting. Do not make the mistake of saving manifesting for „special occasions".

Exercise 7.2: Complex objects - Manifesting a new car

Clicker training the universe may, of course, also be used for manifesting complex objects, such as a new home, car or computer, to just name a few. To do this a little preparation is necessary. You need to get a clear image of what you want into your mind so that the universe can respond to it. In this exercise we will be using a car as an example of a complex manifestation. To prepare, you may want to order some car catalogs from dealerships or simply surf the internet for ideas. The goal is to assemble a list of features your new car should have, such as:

- station waggon
- grey metallic
- leather seats
- less than five years old
- affordable
- non-smoker car
- seat heating

Put down on this list what is important to you. If the brand is important, add it to the list. If you don‘t care about the color, remove it from the list. Your list should be an assembly of those features your car has to have for you to be happy with it. When you have assembled your list, create an image from it in your mind. Then play with that image. In your mind, live through all kinds of situations with it, as if you had it already. Imagine yourself driving in your car and using all its features. Imagine huddling into it on a cold winter morning and turning on the seat heating feeling the heat seep into your body. Imagine driving with some friends to the beach during the summer. Imagine washing it and refuelling it. Imagine driving to your parents singing along to songs from its stereo. Live it! This vivid picture is what you click and treat with strong positive feelings of loving your car and being grateful for it. Imagine it a bit longer, wallow in all the positive feelings associated with your great new car. And then let go and forget about it.

Visuals

When visualizing items, such as a new car, I find it helpful to place photographs of the item in strategic places. You can simply go to the car manufacturer‘s website and copy any images that depict the car you desire. Alternatively, you can cut out photos from the physical catalogue. Print or copy these photos several times and place them in strategic locations, such as:

- on the fridge
- on the front door
- on your desk
- in your wallet
- besides the bathroom mirror
- on your night stand

You may even use them as a screensaver or as a monitor background image. These photos serve to clarify your desires, but also as a reminder to you. Whenever you look at any of those photos think quickly and quietly in your mind‘ „Yes!“, „I love it!“, „Thank you!“ for a little boost to your manifesting efforts.

Exercise 7.3: Fine tuning

Often when you are manifesting, the universe does not provide you with the complete and correct version of what you wanted to manifest right away. Sometimes the universe drops you hints, before it delivers or it will provide what you wanted, but gets certain aspects that are important to you wrong. How you respond to these off-shots is relevant to your manifesting success.

This is no reason to settle for less than what you wanted! It is also not a sign that the universe „thinks“ you don‘t deserve what you want. Please free yourself from such detrimental mind games. In all likelihood you were a little distracted or not quite sure of what you thought you wanted while you were going through your manifestation exercise. Ambivalence about supposedly desired outcomes can show up in interesting ways. Let‘s use home hunting as an example. Imagine you are looking for a new home. You have a detailed list of the features your heart is set on, such as:

- three rooms
- sunny
- grown in backyard with old trees
- close to public transport
- wooden floors
- affordable
- ready to move in
- available immediately
- three bathrooms
- gas powered stove
- floor heating
- nice view
- two parking spots
- nice neighbors

You have been home hunting for months now, but each home you have seen is lacking some important feature. You are so frustrated that the thought of looking at another home, getting your hopes up again for nothing makes your stomach churn. Your deadline for vacating your current home is creeping up on you and you are ready to settle rather than continuing to hope for your dream home. There is a lot of negative energy involved in this for you at this point. What you need to do at this point is to help the universe to get you your dream home. Next time you are going to look at a potential home, go through your feature list beforehand, click & treating each item on the list. After you have arrived at the viewing, feature list set firmly in your mind, focus on those features that the home does have. Do not think: „three rooms: check, sunny: check, Backyard: check“ and then dwell on the home having tiles instead of wooden floors. Instead, your mind-set should be:

- „Three rooms! „Yes!“, „I love it!“, „Thank you!“
- „Sunny! „Yes!“, „I love it!“, „Thank you!“
- „Affordable! „Yes!“, „I love it!“, „Thank you!“

In this way click & treat all the home‘s features that do match your list. Ignore the ones that don‘t. If not enough features match your list for you to want to keep the home, throw it back into the market and trust that a better match will come to you.

8. Your training journal

There will be times where you will get frustrated with training the universe. You will feel, as if you are just not getting anywhere. In these kinds of situations which happen even to experienced manifestors, a training journal is worth its weight in gold.

In it you may read and relive how one manifestation after the other was mastered by you. For the more complex manifestations you are working on, you will be able to see all the signs that clearly show you that your manifestations are well on the way to being created. Luckily for us frustrated manifestors, we then usually realize pretty quickly that the frustration is merely in our heads. Looking back, we have already come a long way. This really helps to beat down frustration and get newly motivated to keep on going. In addition, the training journal will also help to identify manifesting blockages and where they may stem from. You will be able to recognise the patterns, e.g. whether a blockage always arises in similar situations or with similar topics. The more details you note down in your training journal, the more useful a tool it will be for you. This will help you to identify and subsequently chose times, places and situations that make manifesting easiest for you. Perhaps you will notice that after a visit by your mother in law it is impossible for you to manifest anything. Or you may notice that after such a visit you become a manifester extraordinaire. Maybe you react to the full moon, to music, to the time of day or to temperature? Maybe it is easy for you to manifest items, but next to impossible to manifest cash, or the other way around. Usually, such issues can only be discovered, if they are noted down somewhere, as only over time will you be able to recognise the patterns. You may realize which emotional blocks you need to resolve, in order to become a more proficient manifester. Once you have identified the issues, you can start deleting them using methods, such as EFT or psychotherapy.

The format of a training diary is completely up to you. Some trainers only jot down short notes in a little notebook, others prefer a loose leaf collection which they organise in a binder. Others again like to write about their successes and challenges on mailing lists or on an internet message board.

The advantage of the latter can be that you will get loads of feedback. On the one hand, your fellow members will praise you for good work. This is highly motivating. On the other hand many eyes will see more than two. This holds in particular for people who have more emotional distance to your manifesting goals than you. They may notice issues that would never have occurred to you. This can be extremely helpful.

Also when facing a manifesting blockage a group of like minded people is very helpful. Often they will come up with solutions that you never would have dreamt of. Or they can give you a little boost of energy to help you over some manifesting hurdles you may be experiencing. In that a like-minded group can be your manifesting „training wheels". In addition, seeing other peoples" manifesting success can be a boost to by strengthening your belief that it is indeed possible. Finally, posting in a message board helps to keep up a good manifesting discipline. If you won't post for a few days, you can be sure that your new manifesting buddies will want to know what happened and how your manifesting is progressing. This will motivate you to keep going.

9. Chaining

In training, several separate commands may be strung together. This is called chaining and is used to teach complex behaviors. To teach this the trainer takes the complex behavior and separates it into its components. If we use again our yellow ball retrieving example, the training goal is for the dog to retrieve the yellow ball for you. This may be broken down into the following separate exercises:

- running towards an object
- coming to you on command
- picking up an object

- running with an object
- selecting the yellow ball
- coming to you with the yellow ball
- releasing an object to you
- releasing the yellow ball to you

These can all be trained separately, before being chained into one exercise that is executed upon hearing one cue.

The same method may be used for complex types of manifesting. You practice all the parts, string them together and put them onto one command. When you have practiced the chained exercise sufficiently, your mind and soul will go into auto mode when you say your command. This can make manifesting a lot easier.

You already use chaining in everyday life. For example, if you think „home“, what do you see before your inner eye? What to you feel? What do you smell and hear? For me the word „home“ means my house, fireplace crackling, something divine smelling backing in the oven, my dogs running to the door to greet me, warmth, a sense of well being and relaxation. Now that is a lot to think of just by saying one word. Wouldn‘t you agree? I would like to demonstrate the chaining method with a health example:

Exercise 9.1:

Chaining for good health

After having done your warm-up exercises and gotten comfortable, close you eyes and focus on your feet. Imagine them being healthy, beautiful and completely relaxed and well.

If you want, you may also imagine your filled with or enveloped in golden-white light. Feel their well-being in your mind. Then click & treat that visual: „Yes!“ „I love it!“ „Thank you!“. Next, focus on your lower legs. Imagine them being healthy, beautiful, completely relaxed and well. You may also imagine them filled with golden-white light. Then click & treat that visual: „Yes!“ „I love it!“ „Thank you!“. In this way move up your entire body:

- Knees
- Upper legs
- Torso: Remember to include the inner organs: heart, stomach, lungs, womb, liver, kidneys
- Breasts
- Back
- Hands
- Forearms
- Upper arms
- Shoulders

- Neck
- Head

Finally, focus on your entire body at once, imagine it being healthy, beautiful, completely relaxed and well. Imagine it filled and surrounded with golden-white light. Then click & treat that visual: „Yes!“ „I love it!“ „Thank you!“ Practice this once a day for several days. I would suggest a week, as general guideline. But only you know, when you have started to feel completely at home with this exercise. When you do, you should be able to run through it quickly and smoothly, easily calling up each body part.

Once you do, chose a cue word or phrase, like „healthy body“. This you say before you begin the exercise. Then you run through the complete exercise and conclude it with saying “Thank you“ to yourself. This brackets the entire exercise, yielding a clear start and end point. Practice this also for a few days, until you feel that the cue and the exercise are well connected. This means that when you say the cue, the exercise starts running in your mind, as if it were on autopilot. Thus, you use one cue and your body and mind do the rest, saving you time and effort, as you manifest your way to perfect health. This is by the way just a short version. Should you have a lot of time, you can, of course get into a lot more detail while going through your body with this exercise.

For example instead of working on the entire foot, you could start with working on each toe by itself. Then you could work on the forefoot, the midfoot, the heel and the ankle. The lower leg could be split-up into calfs, shins and the muscles inside. Play with it. See what feels good. If, on the other hand, you have little time, you can do this exercise just for sections of your body at the time, e.g. In the morning you do the lower body and in the evening you do the upper body. Or, like a weight lifter, you can work the different parts of your body on alternating days. Just remember to put the different variations of this exercise onto different triggers, such as shoulder-health or upper-body-health.

Exercise 9.2: Chaining for a significant other

The human body provided a great structure for the health exercise, as you worked your way from bottom to top. Unfortunately, this is not the case for most other complex manifestation issues, such as bringing a perfect new mate into your life. I would recommend, therefore, that you sit down before the exercise and write a list of all the characteristics that your new partner should have. Get into as many details, as you wish. There is no right or wrong in this. You should be covering physical, mental and external aspects of your dream partner, such as:

Mental
- sense of humor
- reliable
- faithful
- vegetarian
- animal lover, etc.

Physical
- blue eyed
- healthy
- over 6‘, etc.
- slender

External
- wealthy
- works from home
- popular
- wears nice clothes
- respected by community, etc.

Have fun with this! You should have a big smile on your face, as you are concocting this list. Once you have drawn it up, you may start with the actual exercise. Take the first item on your list, in this case sense of humor, and imagine it really vividly. Imagine how you are joking with each other, laughing enjoying each others company. Imagine, how he makes a mistake and laughs at him self. Imagine you making a mistake, him teasing you laughingly about it and both of you laughing. This should make you feel really good. Make the happiness feeling connected with this aspect from him as big as you can. Then freeze it by click & treating it.

Move to the next item on your list and proceed, until you have worked through the entire list. Do this for several days, until you have memorized the list well and are able to run through the exercise with ease. Then you may introduce your cue word, such as „boyfriend“, as outlined in Exercise 9.1.

Exercise 9.3: Chaining to clear blocks while manifesting

Often we have internal blocks that keep us from manifesting. There are various methods for clearing them. One of those methods can be easily integrated with chaining exercises. The method involves harnessing your subconscious to clear blocks, as they come up. To do this you ask your subconscious to run through the exercise completely and beautifully by

itself when you say the cue word. You request your subconscious to identify and remove all blocks to your manifestation that it encounters while running this exercise.
You set this up by giving you subconscious clear instructions regarding a chained exercise that you have previously trained and connected to a cue. The words you use to program your subconscious could be something like: „Dear subconscious, whenever I say „health“ to you from now on, please run this complete exercise for me. Please find and dissolve any blocks to this exercise that you may be encountering while you are running it. They are irrelevant to us, now, and it is good to let them go. Thank you.“

You can chose other words of course. But whichever words you chose, you need to make sure that the wording is assertive and positive, telling your subconscious clearly what it should do for you. You have probably heard before that it is difficult for your subconscious to understand negations. I would tend to agree with that.

10. Vision boards and videos

In the previous chapters, we have learned to visualize to manifest items and situations we desire. But, what do you do, if you would like to manifest something really complex, such as an entirely new lifestyle? Of course, you could visualize and manifest each item that belongs to your new lifestyle, individually. It is difficult though to hold these items in attention with all the required details at the same time.

Manifesting them in series is not always appropriate. A complete lifestyle is made-up of features that are on the same level in importance and that often are parallel on the time line. Vision boards and videos help us out of this quandary.

What is a vision board?

A vision board is a collage of photos, items and script that show all the important features of what you are manifesting. A vision boards may be made physically with cardboard, plywood or even a scrapbook as basis. Or you can make a virtual vision board using your computer.

Both methods have advantages and disadvantages. It is entirely up to you to decide which you prefer. Alternatively, you could do both or even integrate the approaches. For example you could start off with a virtual vision board and enhance it after printing it out by gluing some physical items to it. Or you could take photos of some physical items, so you could get them onto your virtual clipboard.

Exercise 10.1: Lifestyle board

Many of us have lifestyles that are less than perfect for us. Our ideal lifestyle may be a little or a lot different from the life we currently lead. A vision board is a great way to help manifest a brighter future.

Step 1: Collecting

To prepare for making your vision board, you need to notice and collect pictures and items that fit into your new lifestyle. Skim through magazines and cut out or scan anything that you like, including images, but also headlines or text that you like. You can also surf the internet saving any images you like. If the images cannot be saved directly, you can always make a screenshot and crop the image later to show only what you would like to see using a program such as irfan view. You can also collect any physical items that have significance for your desired life. These can be: coins, flowers, pebbles, fabric swatches, air line tickets or anything else that you want to be a part of your new life.

Step 2: Modifying

Life is not always perfect and neither are the items you have been collecting. Thus, before you start with making your vision board you will need to modify or completely make up any items depicting your new life that you are still missing. Examples of such creative efforts are:

Using a computer

- a photo of your face pasted to a model's body
- short articles written about you, praising your accomplishments

- photograph any physical items that you would like to add to your virtual vision board
- make up a book cover of the book you mean to write
- mock up business cards for your new job or your new company
- a huge check paid out to you
- make wedding invitations

Physically

- address an envelope to yourself
  - at your new dream address
  - at your new dream job
  - as the president of your new company
  - if you want to be married, you could address the envelope to Mr. & Mrs. John Doe or, if you are female, use your new name, not your maiden name
- write out a big cheque to yourself
- write a thank you letter to the universe for giving you your new life

Step 3: Pasting

Once you have enough material assembled, you can start with actually creating your vision board. Before you start this excise, please take the time to raise your „thank you" and „I love it" vibrations first. And now, have some fun! You can be as gaudy, childish, girlish, far out as you like. This is your vision board and your life. If you would like that life to be pink and full of frills: Paste it to your vision board. If you want to be surrounded by models: Paste it to your vision board. If you want to have this absurdly impractical and macho car: Paste it to your vision board. If you wand a Tiffany‘s engagement ring so large you can barely lift your hand: Paste it to your vision board. This is all about you and your wildest dreams and desires.

How you paste the photos and items to your vision board is entirely up to your personal style, as well. The only rule is that it has to make you feel great and all smiley whenever you look at it. You could arrange your photos in an orderly manner on a white background. You could arrange the photos wildly and decorate them with lace, flowers, little hearts or smiley faces. If you would like, you could add some text, such as „I am so happy to be rich and famous“ or „I am so happy that this wonderful woman married me“. There are no limits.

Step 4: Hang it up

Once you are done, you should feel great about your vision board. Hang it up in a place where you can look at it often, such as besides your desk. If you have made a virtual vision board, print out several copies and hang them up them up in strategic spots around your home. My favorite spots are:

- on the fridge
- besides the bathroom mirror
- on the wall beside my desk
- besides the bathtub

I think a great location would also be on my front door so that I would see it every morning as I go to work. But frankly, I don‘t want to explain this to people who enter my home. Their disbelieve, questioning or even criticism would be detrimental for my manifesting vibration. So, I will avoid this. The point is that we want to make this as easy as possible for us. Dealing with other people‘s negativity makes it harder - so I would suggest: Don‘t do it. If you are sharing a home with family, roommates or partner, this can be easier said than done. But you can still work around it. Place the collage in your make-up or shaving kit; into your purse, wallet or briefcase; place it in the back of a book you read, or inside your closet. Be creative, I am sure you can find locations that are not subject to public scrutiny.

Step 5: Apply

Now that your surroundings are loaded with images of your heart‘s desire, you need to reinforce that. Every time you look at your vision board smile, raise your vibration and say or think „Yes!“, „I love it!“ and „Thank you!“ You will find that after doing this a couple of times, you will start to automatically smile and feel good whenever you look at your vision board.

Step 6: When the universe responds

After doing this exercise for a while you will notice that elements of your vision board show up in your real life. The car you want drives by as you are waiting at a traffic light, you see a magazine article on your dream location or it comes up in conversation. You make even start seeing money coming to you unexpectedly or from unusual sources. These are sign that show you that the universe has picked up on your dream. This is great and should make you feel fantastic.

Make sure to click and treat your universe for each such sign by emphatically saying „Yes!“, „I love it!“, „Thank you!“. This reinforces not only your vision board, but the creation of your perfect life at is by and by develops.

What is a vision video?

Even more fun than vision boards are vision videos. Basically, they are several vision boards stacked behind each other. Thus, you have much more space to paste all the features of what you desire. In addition, you can add affirmations, inspiring music and even little videos, such as a clip of a most romantic kiss from a movie or of a little sports car cruising through Monte Carlo. These possibilities allow vision videos to appeal that much more strongly to your heart and emotions which is the reason why they can be very effective.

Exercise 10.2: Lifestyle vision video

Most computers come with some type of free video making software that you can use to make a vision video. For example windows pcs have movie maker, macs have garage band. If you don‘t have any of those or would like software that is really easy to use, you could purchase a special vision video software.

Step 1: Create vision boards for your vision video

Divide the lifestyle you would like to manifest into segments, such as home, partner, family, income, job, friends, location, pets and whatever else you can think of. Next, using your computer, create one or more individual virtual vision boards per segment using the method outlined in exercise 10.1. If one item is really important, you may make one slide containing only that one item. Generally, though, you will want to group items that belong to one life segment, as otherwise your vision video will get too long. A five minute video will be watched by you much more frequently than one that is one hour long. You should keep it short, as you will want to be able to watch your vision video often to maximise its effect.

Step 2: Add the click & treats

Make three copies of each slide, one for the click and another one each for the treats. On the first copy write „Yes!“ in big bold letters that you can easily see, even if you are watching your vision video on a screen as small as your smart phone‘s. The second copy will be augmented with „I love it!“ and the third copy with „Thank you!“. Proceed in the same manner with all other slides for your vision video.

Step 3: Collate your slides into one video

Using your video making software, add all the slides you have made to a new video file in the order in which you would like to view them.

Step 4: Add music

Some programs will let you add music to your video. Music can be a great help in raising your vibrations.

Make sure, though, that the music is uplifting, but not distracting. For this reason instrumental music may be preferable to songs. Of course you can turn down the volume whenever you are watching your manifesting videos in locations where neither the wearing of headphones nor the sound of music would be appropriate.

Step 5: Apply

Once your vision video is completed you can load it onto your phone, iPad, youtube or anywhere else that gives you easy access. Integrate watching it into your daily routine. Convenient times to watch are while waiting or doing mundane tasks, such as:

- while riding on public transport
- while waiting in line
- while brushing your teeth
- while ironing
- while washing the dishes
- while exercising
- while relaxing
- while taking a bath

You see there are plenty of times during each day that you can be watching your vision video. It is a really great way to use some time, since watching your vision video should always make you feel great.

11. Tricks of the trade

There are several tricks I have learned over the years that make manifesting a lot easier. I want to share them here with you for best results.

Not manifesting? Energetic blocks may be the reason

Sometimes people follow all the lessons and are still not manifesting. In my opinion, this is due to resistance to a desired outcome. In chapter x I talked to you about the inner police officer trying to protect you and prevent change. What I am talking about here is similar, but bigger than that.

Due to experiences in the past, often childhood, or believe statements that you have integrated into your being, you may be blocking yourself. In order to successfully manifest, you need to dissolve these blocks. One method that I particularly like and frequently use in my consultations to dissolve such manifesting blocks is an energetic method called EFT. With it you can process energetic blocks that prevent you from reaching your highest potential, including trauma and even illness. For more information on EFT please refer to my website: www.annashiney.com.

The power of groups

Manifesting by oneself can be effective, but in groups it can become downright magical. Manifesting in a group not only benefits from added energies, it frees you from being the only one responsible for the outcome. This allows you to focus on manifesting without the performance pressure and therefrom resulting blocking thoughts. Your approach will be more light hearted and this always works better in manifesting that being too determined and driven. Another benefit is that the members of the group are likely not as attached to the outcome of your desire, as you are. Being unattached is however an important ingredient in manifesting. Thus, it is often easier to manifest for another person then for oneself. Group manifestations really benefit from this.

I am the owner of a pet forum and we use group manifestation frequently for severely ill pets. The results are remarkable. The process is quite simple: one of us „officially“ starts the „witches cauldron“, as we affectionately refer to it. The owner of the ill pet posts a photo of the animal when it was healthy and happy. Whoever wants to help focuses on that image holding it in her mind and sends love energy to it. Thus, we support the visualization of the healthy animal with strong positive energy from several of us. It really is amazing how often the animal that has been thus treated by us improves rapidly after this.

So, if you can, do find a group of like minded friends who can support each other in their manifestations. You do not have to meet in person for this. Internet friendships work just as well. It helps to share visuals, such as photos or vision boards for this, so everyone focusses on the exact thing the applicant desires and not on their own version of it. After all, my dream house may be a far cry away from yours.

Feelings as energy indicator

Pay attention to your feelings. Often you will start feeling tense, uncomfortable, unhappy or anxious before you even realize that you are having negative thoughts. Thus, these feelings are your early warning system that you are focussing on unwanted issues or outcomes. Once you become aware of this, you can immediately switch your focus to a positive outcome that makes you feel great.

Avoid other peoples' disbelief

Don't go around telling everyone about your manifestation efforts. Many will not believe that it is possible. It is not your job to be a missionary. If you speak to disbelievers a lot, their disbelief, negativity, them ridiculing or arguing with you may affect you, making manifesting harder for you. Our goal is, however, to make it as easy as possible. I would therefore recommend that you share your manifestation efforts only with those who believe in manifestation and in you and who will support your efforts.

Feelings journal

In the olden days the great courtesans observed their clients closely and kept journals on them. These journals served for the courtesan to be able to get and keep their client in an amorous mood. In these journals the courtesans noted the client's reaction to a multitude of things: Which foods made the client amorous? Which made him sluggish? Which fragrances enticed him? Which lighting pleased him? Which colors? And so on.

I would suggest for you to become a great courtesan, as well, with her only client being you. What you journal will focus on is the items that put you in a great mood with feelings of love, happiness and gratitude. You should not focus on negative feelings, but if something comes up that kills your good mood, note it and try to avoid it in the future.

What surroundings, foods, temperature, clothing, colors, drinks, etc. get you into a mood that lets you vibrate with positive energy? Integrate as many items from you positive energy journal observations into your everyday life, as possible.

Go through your house, office, car and garden. Go through your entire day, paying attention to how you feel about objects and people. As much as possible, surround yourself with things that make you purr inside like a content pussy cat. Get rid of items that pull you down.

Shopping

When you go clothes shopping, the main question should be no longer: „Do I look fat in this?“ rather it should be: „How do I feel in this?“. Live with your senses! Wear clothing that not only looks good, but rather makes you feel great.
When you go grocery shopping, hold the products in your hands. Look at them. Sniff at them. How do these products feel to you? Do they make you glow, when you let your senses explore them? Those foods will be good for you, make you feel good and will ultimately help you in your manifesting endeavor.

Frustration shopping

Many of us go shopping when we are feeling down. We hope that splurging will make us feel better. Unfortunately, the opposite is true. When we are in a negative energy place, we are drawn to items that fit that energy. Those are items we shouldn‘t even have in our homes. Often, we subconsciously know this and they are forgotten in the back of the closet. My advice to you is: Get rid of them.

Getting rid of stuff

If you have items in your home that you rarely or never use, those are likely items that have negative energy for you. You should clear your house of them, as soon as you can. Luckily those items can have great energy for the person who receives them from you, if given with love in your heart and a big smile. Getting rid of stuff has benefits for you, too. You get rid of negative energy items and make space for positive energy items to come into your home and life. I would suggest that you set the following house rule: For each item that you bring into the house, you have to get rid of at least one negative energy item. By and by your place will be filled with items that carry positive energy and make you feel great.

Feel good file

Sometimes when you are in a slump, it can be difficult to get out of it. A feel good file can really help in these kind of situations.

What is a feel good file?

A feel good file is simply a collection of sign of appreciation from others that makes you feel good about yourself. I know that many spiritual teacher teach you that your appreciation for yourself should come from within. But frankly, that is not the way most of us where raised. Thus, until we get to the point where we are free from all this, there is nothing that can make us feel better more quickly than appreciation from others.

A feel good file might be a folder on your computer or a physical storage device like a box, file folder or pretty diary. My own feel good file is a folder in my googlemail account. That way I can access it pretty much always, whenever or wherever I need it.

Any written communication about you that makes you feel good about yourself, should go into your feel good file. This may be a recommendation letter from a client, a praise from your boss, a friend telling you how much they appreciated your help, or whatever else that makes you smile.

At work this may be emails or letters from clients, colleagues or your boss that praise you. Privately, this may be any written communication that you have received that makes you feel really good about yourself. Should you have no written communications whatsoever, then another option would be to write a memo to yourself about something that happened that made you feel appreciated and validated. Receiving such a communication from others, however, has a lot more impact for most of us.

Harnessing negative emotions

Being human, not matter how much we focus on being positive, there is a good chance that life will wallop us occasionally. This may lead to strong negative emotions, like anger, hate, grief. Usually, we would try to dissipate those negative emotions as quickly as possible to avoid drawing more negative experiences into out life. However, we may also harness those emotions for our manifestations.

Negative emotions are such a strong, pure force of nature. I feel it is a bit of a shame to waste them. Mind you, you do have to be disciplined when using negative emotions in this way. You do not want to be those negative emotions, just because you are holding them. You need to separate yourself from the negative emotions. You hold them, but you are not those negative emotions. That way, you will be able to send them on their way with your manifestation item.

In order to harness the negative emotions, think of an item you would like to manifest. Create a vivid image in your mind that contains all of the item‘s desired features. Once, you have a clear image, shoot all that negative energy you have churning in you at that image. For extra emphasis, I tend to exhale sharply as I do so. Then mentally give the image and the negative emotions a slight push to float them away from you and into the universe. When that is done, take a deep breath. At this point you should be secretly smiling, again. You have a lot to smile about, because:

- the person or situation that made you so upset actually ended up actually helping you to create your wishes. Wouldn‘t they hate that. And don‘t you just love it.
- you just send a lot of energy towards the manifestation of your wish
- the negative emotions are gone
- you were able to put all those negative emotions to such good use

12. The end

Where does the journey go from here? The more you practice the more clicker training will be integrated into your life. There comes a point for each trainer at which she no longer has clearly defined training sessions, only, but instead lives clicker training. These are the people that seem to have well behaved animals without ever actually training them.

In a way this is true. They do not have formal training sessions. But, since they live clicker training, the animal receives ongoing feedback about its behavior. In particular, the animal is rewarded whenever he shows a behavior that is pleasing to his owner.

To an outsider it seems that the animal is virtually training itself. In reality, though, the opposite is true. The animal‘s behavior is shaped non-stop to evolve in the desired direction. The trainer does not even think about it anymore. She loves her animal and her animal loves her, because their relationship is based on positive interactions. Giving the correct responses has become so ingrained that she rewards her dog as automatically and naturally as breathing or walking. Only for special tricks, will such a trainer resort to formal training sessions. But these too will be short, easy and fun.

Clicker training the universe evolves similarly. Stick with it and continue to live it in your day to day life. Then you too will get to the point where you don‘t need to consciously train anymore. You will automatically focus your desires and emotions so that your life seemingly unconsciously evolves into an ever improving reality. Whenever a specific desire presents itself, you will automatically focus on it briefly and send it positive energy. Thus, you will easily and effortlessly manifest your wish.

Remember: Dog is God - only spelled the other way around. As in all training: the trainer is really training himself and not the pupil. You are God. You create your own reality.

If you enjoyed the exercises in this book, please do come to my website. It is a mixture between a blog and an exercise book in which I post my musings about life combined with weekly exercises to integrate a more positive and life enhancing approach into your routine. I hope to see you there.

Have fun training,

Anna G. Shiney

ps. I would love to hear back from you regarding your training successes. Please send an e-mail to anna@annashiney.com or leave a comment on my website.

Who am I?

I, like you, am many things and have done many things. Here are some of those things that define me:

- I have been manifesting for more than 30 years
- I have been an investment banker for more than 20 years
- I have been a clicker trainer for more than 10 years
- I have been a published writer for more than 5 years
- I am a chemical engineer
- I love my parrots and dogs
- I love to sing
- I love making others laugh
- I love to construct things
- I love life

I have also experienced several major life challenges and through them grew to be a deeper, more mature, humble and loving person. I am a living example that both, EFT and the Law of Attraction, do work and that they are invaluable tools for human healing and development. If you think you could benefit from personal coaching with me, please see my website for more information:

www.annashiney.com

www.ingramcontent.com/pod-product-compliance
Lightning Source LLC
LaVergne TN
LVHW051425080426
835508LV00022B/3245